REALLY

DRINKING
JOKES

REALLY WICKED

Other titles in this series:

REALLY WICKED

DRINKING JOKES

Compiled by David Brown

MICHAEL O'MARA BOOKS LTD

First published in Great Britain in 1998
by Michael O'Mara Books Limited
9 Lion Yard
Tremadoc Road
London SW4 7NQ

A CIP catalogue record for this book is available from the British Library

ISBN 1-85479-374-8

3 5 7 9 10 8 6 4 2

Cover design by Powerfresh

Designed and typeset by Design 23

Printed and bound in Great Britain by Cox & Wyman, Reading, Berks.

DRUNK

AND

DISORDERLY

Sitting beside Ben in the pub was the ugliest woman he'd ever set eyes on. In fact, she was so ugly that he'd refused every single one of her sexual advances.

After a couple of hours the woman turned to Ben and said, "Y'know. mishter, if I have one more drink I'm really going to feel it."

"T'tell you the truth, if I have one more drink I prob'ly won't mind!" he replied.

The drunk was staggering along the road with a large bottle of booze in each pocket, when he suddenly tripped and fell heavily to the ground.

As he was pulling himself to his feet he noticed that his trousers felt wet. He touched the wet patch with his fingers, looked blearily at them and sighed, "Thank goodnesh! It'sh only blood."

A stranger walks into a bar and the locals ask him if he wants to play a game of bar football. He says "Sure! What do I have to do?"

The locals said "Drink Beer, Piss, then Fart".

So the stranger picks up the mug and downs the beer, then takes a piss, and lets out an enormous fart.

Then the locals said, "If you can do it again, you get an extra point."

So the stranger picks up the mug again and downs his beer, drops his pants to take a piss, but before he can fart, a local shoves his large finger up the stranger's ass.

The stranger asked "What the Hell are you doing?"

"Blocking the extra point," the local replied.

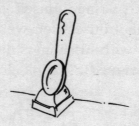

A guy walks into a bar in a high rise block late one evening, orders a beer and then walks over to admire some really strange paintings on the wall. As he is looking at the paintings another gentleman walks over and comments on the art.

"These paintings are really something, aren't they?"

"Why yes, they are quite remarkable. I have never seen anything like them before."

"You know there are other remarkable things about this bar also. You see that window over there? The way the wind currents work, if you jump out of the window, it will blow you right back into the bar. Why don't you give it a try?"

"That's impossible and crazy!"

"Look I'll show you."

The guy jumps out of the window and falls 10ft, 20ft, 30ft, 40ft, 50ft ... and then whooop! ... he stops in mid air and gets blown right back up into the window.

Now the other gentleman is dumbfounded.

"That's amazing. How did you do that?"

"I told you, it's the wind currents. Look I'll show you again."

The guy jumps out of the window and falls 10ft, 20ft, 30ft, 40ft, 50ft ... and then whooop!... he stops in mid air and gets blown right back up into the window.

This time the guy is even more impressed. He cannot believe his own eyes, but he saw it! So he decides to give it a try. He jumps out the window and falls 10ft, 20ft, 30ft, 40ft, 50ft, 60ft, 70ft, 80ft, 90ft ... and then SPLAT!

The other gentleman walks back to the bar, and the barman says,

"Gee, Superman, you can be a real asshole when you're drunk!"

Mike and John got drunk and went fishing one day. They were amazed to discover that they had caught a Genie's bottle. The Genie said he would grant one wish.

Mike said, "I wish all this water around the boat was beer."

The wish was granted and the whole lake turned into beer.

Then John said, "You've really gone and done it now, Mike! Now we'll have to piss in the boat."

A commuter approached the guard: "This morning I accidentally left a bottle of Scotch on the train. Was it handed in to the lost and found by any chance?"

"No," replied the guard, "but the man who found it was!"

DANGEROUS

COCKTAILS

An attractive young lady walked into a working class bar and said to everyone in the bar that she had a riddle for them to answer. If no-one could answer the riddle everyone had to buy her a beer but if someone were able to answer it they would get to have sex with her.

The lady said,

"If my pussy should sail out to sea how would you get it back for me?"

No-one in the bar could give her an answer, so everyone there bought her a beer.

The next night she went to a middle-class bar with the same offer. Again no-one had an answer for her, so everyone bought her a beer.

The next night she entered an upper-class bar, again with the same riddle and the same offer. After a couple of minutes an old man stood up and said,

"If that time should come to pass I'd tie my balls onto my ass, use my cock as an oar and float your pussy back to shore."

She was an attractive barmaid so he slapped a tenner on the bar and said, "I bet I can keep an eye on this drink while I go to the gents."

She knew the gents' loo was around the corner, so she accepted the bet. He took his glass eye out, placed it beside the glass and went to the gents.

"Betcha I can bite my own ear," he challenged. The bet was accepted and he took out his false teeth and nipped his ear. Once more he scooped up the money.

"Okay," he said, "I'll give you a chance to win your money back. I bet I can make love to you so tenderly you won't feel a thing." Now that was one thing she really did know about. So she accepted the bet. He lifted her skirt and away they went.

"I can feel you," she cried.

"Oh well," he said, "You win some, you lose some!"

There was a black man, a white man, and a Mexican sitting in a bar, all drunk. The black guy says to the white guy, "I bet you my cock is bigger than yours."

The white guy says, "No way, mine is bigger than yours."

The Mexican, overhearing the conversation, comes over and says, "No, mine is bigger than both of yours," and starts laughing.

All three of them carried on drinking and arguing.

The white guy comes up with a solution. He says, "We'll all pull our cocks out and put them on the table. That way, we'll see whose is bigger."

All of them agreed and took their cocks out. While they were looking at each other's cocks and comparing them, one of them said, "So, whose is bigger?" None of them could figure it out because they couldn't see straight and were drunk.

While they were standing there, a gay guy walks in and says, "Ohhh Buffet."

A man walks into a New York bar and asks the bartender for a shot of forty-year-old Scotch. Not wanting to go down to the basement and deplete his supply of the rare and expensive liquor, the bartender pours a shot of ten-year-old Scotch and figures that his customer won't be able to tell the difference.

The man downs the Scotch and says, "Hey, that Scotch is only ten-years-old. I specifically asked for forty-year-old Scotch."

Amazed, the bartender reaches into a locked cabinet underneath the bar and pulls out a bottle of twenty-year-old Scotch and pours the man a shot.

The customer drinks it down and says, "That was twenty-year-old Scotch. I asked for forty-year-old Scotch."

So the bartender goes into the back room and brings out a bottle of thirty-year-old Scotch and pours the customer a drink. By now a small crowd has gathered around the man and is watching anxiously as he downs the latest drink. Once again the man states the true age of the Scotch and repeats his original request.

The bartender can hold off no longer and disappears into the cellar to get a bottle of prime forty-year-old Scotch.

As the bartender returns with the drink, an old drunk, who had been watching the proceedings with interest, leaves the bar and returns with a full shot glass of his own.

The customer downs the Scotch and says, "Now this is forty-year-old Scotch!" The crowd applauds his discriminating palate.

"I bet you think you're real smart," slurs the drunk. "Here take a swig of this."

Rising to the challenge, the man takes the glass and downs the drink in one swallow. Immediately, he chokes and spits out the liquid on the bar floor.

"My God!" he exclaims. "That's piss!"

"Great guess," says the drunk. "Now tell me how old I am."

SIMPLE MISTAKES

A white horse walks into a pub, pulls up a stool, and orders a pint of lager. The landlord serves him his beer and says, "You know, we have a drink named after you."

To which the white horse replies, "What, Eric?"

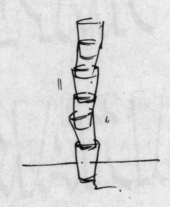

A heavy-drinking New Yorker saw a sign that said "Drink Canada Dry" ... so he went there.

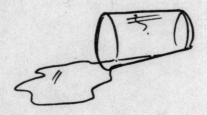

Two drunks met in a bar.

"What's the date, Jimmy?" asked one.

"Dunno," replied Jimmy.

"Well, look at that newspaper in your pocket."

"No use," said Jimmy. "It's yesterday's."

Two men were in a pub, doing some heavy boozing. They were drinking doubles and triples, buying rounds and generally having a good time. When asked why they were celebrating, they boasted that they had just finished a jigsaw puzzle and it had only taken them two months.

"TWO MONTHS," exclaimed the barman, "That absurd. It shouldn't take anywhere near that long."

"Well," said one of the men, "The box said two to four years."

The fire engine careered around the corner and whizzed off up the road, bells clanging, just after a drunk staggered out of a pub. He promptly started chasing after it, but collapsed, exhausted and weeping after only a few hundred yards. "All right," he sobbed, "You can keep your rotten ice lollies!"

There were two deaf drunks travelling on the tube:

First drunk: "Is this Wembley?"

Second drunk: "No, it's Thursday."

First drunk: "So am I, let's get out and have one!"

A man walked into a pub and demanded to be served a drink called 'Less'.

"I've never heard of it." said the barmaid.

"You must have heard of it!" insisted the man

"Well, we don't stock it, I'm afraid. Is 'Less' a new, foreign beer or something? Where did you hear about it?" asked the barmaid.

"I don't know exactly what it is," replied the man, "but my doctor insists that I drink 'Less'."

A six-year-old boy walks into a pub, climbs up onto a stool and says, "Give me a Scotch on the rocks."

"You're just a child!" the barmaid says. "Do you want to get me into trouble?"

"Maybe later," the boy replies. "In the meantime, I'll have that drink."

In a small, rural village, the local drunk is weaving his way up the main street. The local vicar, a rather harsh man, famed for his puritanical views, is watching his progress with a disdainful eye. The drunk spots him and lurches over. "Your Holynesh, you're my besht mate. How the hell are you?"

This combination of drunkenness and profanity is too much for the vicar who explodes, "Drunk! And on a Sunday!"

"Your shecret's shafe with me, Reverend. To tell the truth, I've had a couple of quick ones myself."

Two young men are sitting in a disco, both pretty drunk, when one of them notices a beautiful woman standing on her own in the corner. "Wow!" he says to his mate, "I'd love to dansh with her."

"Go and ashk her, then, don't be a chicken." said the mate.

So the first man goes over and says, "Excushe me, Mish, would you like to dansh with me?"

Seeing that he is totally drunk and rather

inexperienced, the woman says, "I'm sorry – right now I'm concentrating on matrimony and I'd rather sit than dance."

The young man returns to his mate looking really put down.

"What did she say, then?" he asks.

"She said she's constipated on macaroni and would rather shit in her pants," came the reply.

At the end of his shift, the Aussie barman turns on the TV in the London pub where he's working to catch the highlights of the day's play in the Ashes.

There is only one drinker in the pub and he becomes equally engrossed in the game. When the Aussie pace bowler bowls out one of the England openers, the drinker puts it down to luck. When, with his next ball, the same bowler clean bowls the incoming batsman, the drinker is outraged at the 'fluke'.

Such is his indignation that he bets the barman £10 that the bowler won't get a hat-trick. The barman has seen that part of the game earlier and accepts the bet, knowing full well that the bowler does get his hat trick.

They watch the third ball, the drinker bellows in disbelief and hands over the tenner to the guilt-stricken barman.

"No, I can't take your money, mate. I watched it live this afternoon."

"So did I," replied the drinker. "I just didn't think he'd able to pull it off twice in a row."

A drunk goes into a pub and sees a jar filled with £20 notes on the bar. The barman explains that it costs £20 to enter the pub competition. All he has to do is three things:

First, knock out the other barman who is a huge seven-footer and 18 stone.

Second: there is a vicious 13-stone rottweiler out in the back alley with toothache and he must extract the tooth.

Third: there is an old prostitute upstairs who has never had an orgasm and he must sort her out.

"I'll have a go," says the drunk.

He walks up to the monstrous barman and, 'BANG', knocks him out stone cold.

He then goes out to the back alley and there's all sorts of barking, yelping, howling and the like – the poor dog's agony is unbelievable.

After about half an hour the drunk returns and says,

"Right that's that, now where's this old prostitute with toothache."

A man walks into a pub and notices he's the only one there, apart from the barman, who's on the phone. The barman signals him that he'll be with him in a minute. The man nods, sits on a stool and waits to be served.

Suddenly, he hears a little voice say, "Hello, you're looking rather smart today. New suit?"

The man looks around but can't see anyone else in the place. He hears the voice again. "Seriously... THAT is a fabulous tie, chum!" The man looks around again and still doesn't see anyone.

"Hello?" he asks. "Is someone speaking to me?"

"Absolutely! I just have to say you look marvellous! Have you lost weight?"

A crowd of other tiny voices suddenly chorused in agreement. The man realizes now that these voices are coming from a bowl of peanuts on the bar in front of him. He stares at them as the barman finally hangs up and comes to serve his only customer.

"What'll you have?" asks the barman.

"What?... Oh, a pint of bitter, I suppose," mutters the man, still staring at the peanuts. He finally looks up at the barman drawing his pint.

"What's about these nuts?" he asks.

The barman brings the man's pint over and sets it before him.

"Oh, the nuts? They're complimentary!"

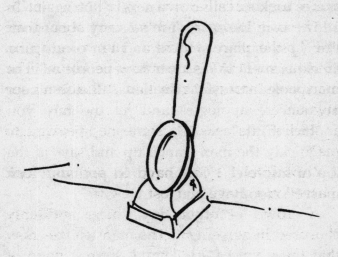

A man is minding his own business in his local pub, drinking a pint of beer, when a gorgeous looking girl comes in, sits down beside him and gives him a stunning smile. Just as he's thinking up his opening line, she says in a loud, indignant voice that everyone can hear, "Your place? Certainly not!" and she gets to her feet and moves to the other end of the bar.

He sits there feeling completely embarrassed, imagining what everyone is thinking of him and wondering how he can ever live this down. After a while the girl comes back and sits down next to him again. In a low voice she says, "I'm so sorry about that. I'm a psychology student and I'm conducting an experiment to discover how people react to unexpected stressful situations. Please accept my sincere apologies and let me buy you another drink."

Quickly the man stands up and says at the top of his voice, "One hundred pounds? You must be bloody joking!"

A man walks into a bar and sits down next to a sailor whose head is about the size of an orange. The man and the sailor begin to talk and after ten minutes, curiosity got the better of the man and he asked, "How did you get that tiny head of yours?" And so the sailor began.....

"When I was in the navy, my ship sank and I was the only survivor. I swam to a nearby deserted isle and, when I arrived, I heard a woman yelling for help.

I found a mermaid stranded on the beach. She was the most beautiful woman I ever saw! I carried her to the water and she said, 'For your generosity I will grant you three wishes.'

Of course, I accepted.

'MY FIRST WISH,' I said, 'Will be to be FILTHY RICH.' A huge box of jewels appeared on the sand.

'MY SECOND WISH will be to get home safely.' And a golden yacht with beautiful women on it appeared on the horizon, headed for the island.

'MY THIRD WISH will be to make love to you,' I said.

'Well,' she replied, 'as you can see, I'm not really built for that sort of thing.'

'Then how about just a little head?'."

A punk with a multicoloured mohawk, spiky hairdo goes into a pub to have a couple of beers. After a while he notices an old man at the other end of the bar, staring at him. Every time he looks up this man is still staring.

Finally he can't take it any more, so he goes over to the man and says, "Why are you staring at me? Haven't you ever done anything weird in your life?

The old man says, "I certainly have done some weird things in my life. As a matter of fact, I had sex with a peacock once, and I was wondering if you were my son!"

A juggler, driving to his next performance, was stopped by the police.

"What are those knives doing in your car?" asked the officer.

" I juggle them in my act," he replied.

"Oh yes?" says the policeman. "Let's see you do it."

So the juggler starts tossing and juggling the knives.

A man driving by sees this and says, "God, am I glad I stopped drinking. Look at the test they're making you do now!"

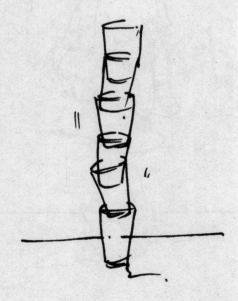

DRUNKEN

LOGIC

A horse walks into a bar, pulls up a stool, and orders a beer.

The barman asks, "Why the long face?"

A pony walks into a bar.

The barman says, "What's the matter with you?"

"Nothing, really! I'm just a little horse!"

How did two drunk gays in a pub settle their argument?

They went outside and exchanged blows.

What do you say to a couple of martinis?

I never speak to them.

A man walks into a pub and says, "Can I have an entendre please?"

"Would that be a single or a double?" asks the barmaid.

"Oh, make it a double," he replies.

"So yours is a large one, then sir," she says.

A drunk stumbled upon a man looking under the bonnet of his car.

"What's the matter?" mumbled the drunk.

"Oh, piston broke," replied the motorist.

"Me too," said the drunk.

It seems that the correct behaviour at cocktail parties is to only open your mouth when you have nothing to say.

A man walked into a bar in Cairo, went up to the barman and ordered a drink. As the barman was pouring it, he looked at the customer and said, "Haven't you been in here before, Sir?"

"Once or twice." replied the customer.

"I thought so," said the barman, "I can't remember your name, but I've definitely seen your fez before."

A man was struggling to carry a big grandfather clock up the steps into his house when he was hailed by a drunk.

"Take my advish, mishter – get yershelf a wrisht watch."

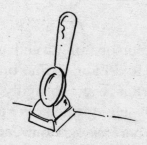

A man walks into a pub and says to the barman, " I'll have a Scotch and soda and I'd like to buy that douche bag at the end of the bar a drink."

"Watch your mouth," the barman says.

"You can't just come in here and start talking about people like that!"

"Well, O.K. then," says the man, "I'd like to buy that nice young lady at the end of the bar a drink."

"That's better." the barman says, and walking over to the girl, he asks her what she'd like to drink.

"Vinegar and water, please," she says.

An Elvis impersonator turned up to perform his set at the Red Lion, to find only two people sitting in what was normally a very well attended pub. He stormed over to the landlord and said, "Where the hell is everyone tonight?"

"I've no idea," replied the landlord. "It must just be a slow night."

"Did you tell all your regulars I was playing here?"

"No. Sorry, it must have just slipped out!"

What's the difference between a fox and a dog?
Half a dozen large whiskies.

On the chest of a barmaid from Sale
Were tattooed the prices of ale.
And on her behind
For the sake of the blind,
Was the same information in Braille.

Ned had been warned that he must be on his best behaviour when his wealthy aunt arrived for a brief visit. At tea time on the first day of her stay, Ned kept staring at his aunt, and finally, when they were all nearly finished, he asked, excitedly, "Auntie, when are you going to do your trick?"

"What trick is that, Ned?" she enquired.

"Well," he replied, "Daddy says you can drink like a fish."

What do American beer and making love in a canoe have in common?

They're both f**king close to water.

Q: What is the difference between a toilet and a barman?
A: A toilet only has to deal with one asshole at a time!

"What do you drink?"
"Whisky and carrot juice."
"Weird mixture."
"Well, you get drunk just as fast and you can see where you're going to fall."

What's the difference between an alcoholic and a drunk?

If you're rich you're an alcoholic and if you're poor you're just a drunk.

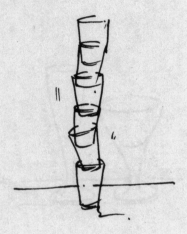

What's the difference between a drunk and an alcoholic?

A drunk doesn't have to go to meetings.

LAW

AND

ORDER

One day while on patrol, a policeman pulled over a car for speeding. He went up to the car and asked the driver to roll down her window. The first thing he noticed, apart from the fancy red sports car, was how attractive the driver was. Long blonde hair, fantastic figure, she really was the bee's knees.

"I've pulled you over for speeding, madam. Could I see your licence please?" said the policeman.

"What's a licence? replied the blonde, instantly giving away the fact she was as thick as a plank.

"It's usually in your wallet," replied the officer. After fumbling for a few minutes, the girl managed to find it.

"Now can I see your insurance details?" asks the copper.

"Insurance details? What are they?" she asked.

"They're usually in the glove compartment," said the copper, growing impatient. After some more fumbling, she found her insurance details.

"I'll be back in a minute," said the copper and walked back to his car. He radioed in to

run a check on the woman's details and, after a few moments the control room came back to him.

"Is this woman driving a red sports car?" asked the voice over the radio.

"Yes," said the copper.

"Is she a really sexy looking blonde?"

"Uh, yes," replied the copper.

"In that case, give her back her licence and insurance and drop your trousers."

"WHAT?" shrieked the copper, "I can't do that."

"Trust me, just do it," said the man in the control room.

So the policeman goes back to the car, gives the girl back her documents and drops his trousers. The blonde looks down and sighs, "Oh, no... not ANOTHER breathalyser."

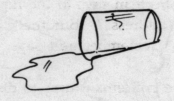

Two old drunks come stumbling out of a pub and start pissing in a nearby garden. A policeman comes along and takes them in on charges of indecent exposure. Writing up the charge, the policeman says to the first drunk, "What's your address?" But the man is so drunk he can't remember and says, "I don't know."

Irritated, the policeman turns to the second drunk, "Well, where do you live?"

"I live next door to him." comes the reply.

Late one night the police were following a car. The driver was driving immaculately, never exceeding the speed limit, giving all the correct signals and even being courteous to other drivers.

Eventually the police car came alongside him, indicating that he should pull over. "Good evening, Sir," the officer said, "Don't be alarmed, you aren't in any trouble – we just wanted to compliment you on your exemplary driving."

"Thank you, officer," replied the driver. "I always make a point of driving carefully at night, especially when I've had a few pints."

Two policemen walked over to a drunk lying on the beach.

"We're looking for a drowned man," they said.

"You don't shay," said the surprised man. "Whatcha want one for?"

A rabbi and a priest were involved in a car accident, and it was a bad one. Both cars were totally demolished but, amazingly, neither of the men were hurt. After they crawled out of the wrecks, the rabbi noticed the priest's collar and said,

"Well, you're a priest and I'm a rabbi and just look at our cars. They are both write-offs but we've escaped unhurt. It must be God's will. He must have intended us to meet, become friends and live alongside each other in peace for the rest of our days."

"I absolutely agree with you." the priest replied. "this is certainly a sign from God."

"And just look at this," the rabbi continued, "here's another miracle! My car is totalled but this bottle of kosher wine didn't break. Surely God wants us to celebrate our good fortune with a drink." And he handed the bottle of wine to the priest who took a few, big swigs and handed the bottle back. The rabbi put the cork back in and threw the bottle as far away as he could into the woods.

"Aren't you having any?" asked the priest.

"No," replied the rabbi. "I think I'll wait for the police."

An Irishman was brought up before the judge. "Why were you drunk?" the judge asked.

"I was on a train with bad companions." replied the Irishman. "Four teetotallers."

"But they are the best company you could keep!" exclaimed the judge.

"I don't think so, your Honour. I had a bottle of whisky about my person and I had to drink it all by myself."

A policeman sees a car weaving all over the road and pulls it over. He walks up to the car and can smell alcohol on the breath of the attractive lady driver.

He says, "I'm going to have to give you a breathalyser test to see if you are under the influence of alcohol."

She blows into the bag and he walks back to the police car. After a couple of minutes he returns and says, "It looks like you've had a couple of stiff ones."

"Good gracious," she exclaims, "you mean it shows that too?"

The policeman was on the witness stand.

"I could see him in the middle of the road on his hands and knees."

"Your honour," interrupted the lawyer. "Just because a man is in the middle of the road on his hands and knees at midnight is no sign that he is drunk."

"What the counsel for the defence says is quite true," agreed the policeman. "But the defendant was trying to roll up the white line."

DRINKS ON THE HOUSE

A travelling salesman goes into a country pub to find a great big glass jar full of £5 notes on the bar. "Put five pounds in," explains the barman. "To win the lot all you have to do is to make the donkey in the back paddock laugh."

The salesman pays up, goes out the back and whispers in the donkey's ear, and with that the donkey laughs and laughs and laughs. The salesman grabs the money and goes.

Next year the same thing happens all over again. The salesman whispers, gets the money and goes.

The next year however, the clever barman advises the salesman that the rules have all changed. This year he must make the donkey cry.

Out goes the salesman and the next thing you know the donkey is crying and sobbing uncontrollably, tears rolling off the end of his nose.

The salesman is about to leave with the money again, when the barman says to him, "That's three years in a row you've got the money. Tell me how the bloody hell did you do it?"

"Easy," says the salesman. "First two years I

simply whispered to him that my cock was much bigger than his."

"Yes" said the barman, "what about this year."

"Simple again," said the salesman, "I showed it to him."

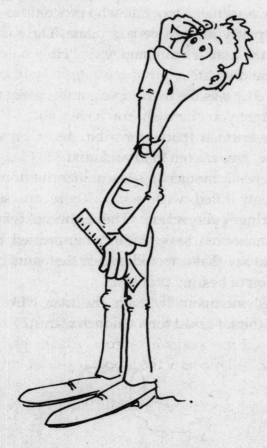

A man walks into a pub and says to the barman, "If I can really amaze you, will you give me a free drink?"

The barman, confident that he seen it all, agrees, and then is completely stunned when the man reaches into his bag and produces a piano player, less than a foot tall, who proceeds to play some pretty impressive jazz piano. The barman gives the man a drink and says, "How on earth did you do that?"

"Well," says the man, "I've got this genie who will grant you one wish. You have a go!"

The barman thinks for a bit, and then says, "Genie, give me ten thousand quid."

There's a moment's silence, then the room is suddenly filled with squid. There are squid slithering everywhere. The barman, who is clearly shocked, says, "Well I'm impressed, but I have to say that it would appear that your genie has a bit of hearing problem."

"Tell me about it," says the man, "Do you really think I asked for a ten-inch pianist?"

A guy walks over to a barman and offers him a bet. "I bet you £100 that I can go over to the corner of the bar and piss into this mug right here in my hand with out making a single drop. In other words in the glass and only the glass."

So, the guy goes into the corner and unzips his flies. And he's saying in his mind, 'Dick, Glass, Dick, Glass...'

So after a few minutes he starts to piss. He's pissing everywhere – on the barman, on the tables across from him, even in other people's drinks. In fact he's pissing everywhere BUT the glass!

So when he's done, the barman is standing there laughing, with piss all over his face and dripping off his chin.

The barman says, "You idiot. You just lost £100!"

And the guy says, "Well, see those guys over there? I bet them £250 that I could piss on you and you wouldn't get angry. I also said that by the time I was finished, you would be laughing!"

HUSBANDS AND WIVES

My husband isn't a hard drinker – he finds it very easy!

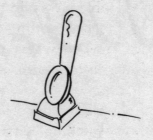

A couple were dining out in a smart restaurant when the wife noticed a familiar face at the bar.

"Thomas," she said, pointing, "do you see that man downing cognacs at the bar?" Her husband looked over and then nodded. "Well," said the woman, "He's been drinking like that for ten years now, ever since I left him."

Her husband started eating again. "Rubbish," he said, "even that's not worth that much celebrating."

There I was at the office Christmas party, in my expensive new suit, anxious to impress my new boss. The only problem was my wife who kept going over to the bar, getting a new drink, bringing it back to where we were standing and drinking it down in one with her back to the bar.

By the time she was on her seventh, I noticed that my boss was watching her. I really wanted to go after her but I was stuck in a tedious conversation with someone from the computer systems department. From the corner of my eye I could see my boss had started talking to my wife. He smiled at her. She smiled at him. He frowned and she walked back towards me.

Finally the computer systems man moved on to bore someone else and I said, "Darling, what did my boss say to you? Did he mention how many drinks you've had? You aren't doing my career much good, behaving like this. He'll think you've got a drink problem."

"No, he won't," replied my wife. "He certainly doesn't think I've got a drink problem. I'm not a liability to you, darling. I just told him you keep sending me to the bar to get you more to drink."

A drinker rolled home late on a Friday night, and as he walked in, there was his wife with her hand outstretched.

"OK!" she said. "Where's your pay packet? Hand it over!"

With a guilty look on his face, he pulled it out of his pocket and handed it over saying, "You'll find it's not all there. I spent half of it on something for the house."

"Oh, that's nice," she said, "What was it?"

"A round of drinks," he replied.

A man drinks a few whiskies every night before going to bed. After years of this his wife wants him to quit, so she gets two shot glasses, fills one with water, the other with whisky. She places the glasses on the table and gets her husband to fetch his fishing-bait box.

"I want you to watch this carefully," she says and puts a worm in the water and it swims around. She then takes the worm out and puts it in the whisky where it dies.

"So," she says. "What do you have to say about this experiment?"

"Well," he says. "If I drink whisky I won't get worms."

During World War II, a couple of American soldiers stationed in England, discovered a local pub, whose house speciality was called 'Half & Half', a mixture of two different beers. At closing time, the two Americans didn't want to leave, but the publican was insistent.

After locking the door and going upstairs, the publican and his wife were unable to get to sleep as the two drunk Americans kept beating on the pub door and yelling, "We won't leave until you give us some more of that Half & Half!"

Finally the publican could stand it no longer. He reached under the bed, removed the chamberpot, and opened the window. As he emptied the pot on the two drunks, he cried, "Ere's your bloody 'alf and 'alf! 'Tis 'alf mine and 'alf the old lady's!"

A married couple got some beers at the bar. After their beers were served, the man took his back to the counter. After telling the barmaid why he wasn't happy with his beer, she slapped his face. When his wife asked why she slapped him, he replied "I only asked her for some head."

A man comes home, very late, pissed out of his mind, to find his wife waiting for him at the door.

"WHERE HAVE YOU BEEN?" she screams. "It's 4 a.m."

He says, "Aww, I just stopped at this bar, I was only going to have one beer... but this bar, it was incredible. EVERYTHING in it was gold plated. They had a gold rail under the bar, gold ashtrays, they served the drinks in gold glasses, the table legs were all gold-plated, even the mirror behind the bar was gold. The cash register was gold.

I was so amazed by all this gold, I just kept on ordering beers, so I could stay in the bar and look at it. Hell, even when I went to the loo to piss, they had gold plated urinals....it was wonderful."

"I don't believe that story for one minute," his wife said. "What was this place called?"

"Hell," he replies, "I can't remember...I got too drunk, and I forgot." "You'll have to prove it to me tomorrow when you sober up, or I'm going to divorce you!" she said.

The next day, the man looks through the Yellow Pages under BARS, but none of the names ring a bell. He decides that he'll call all the bars listed, and ask the bartenders about the decor in their establishments. He's called about fifty bars so far, and still no luck. Finally he calls one bar, asks his question, and the barman says that, yes, they are the bar with all these gold plated things.

"Here," the man says, handing the phone to his wife, "Ask the barman if I'm lying!"

The wife gets on the line, and begins to ask the barman about all the things her husband

had told her about on the previous night....the rail, the glasses, the mirrors, the table legs and the cash register. Finally, she says, "Now, this may seem like a strange question, but my husband says you even have gold-plated urinals...do you?"

The barman puts the phone down on the bar, and she hears him yell, "HEY LOUIE! I think I know who pissed in your saxophone....."

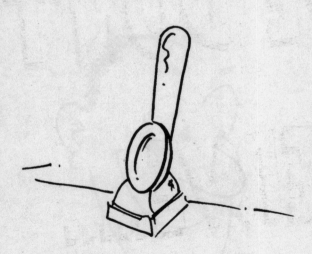

SORRY, WE DON'T SERVE.....

A length of rope was walking down the street and, feeling a bit thirsty, it popped into a pub. "Excuse me," it said to the landlord, "I'd like a pint of bitter, please."

The landlord looked at it and replied, "Aren't you a .... rope?"

"Yes, I am." said the rope.

"Well, get out of here!" said the landlord. "I'm not going to serve beer to a rope!"

Feeling rather miserable, the rope left and a little further down the street it spotted a second pub. In it went, sat down on a stool, and asked the barman for a pint.

"Hang on," said the barman, "Aren't you a ... rope?"

"Yes, but I can pay –"

"No, way!" snapped the barman. "We don't cater to ropes in this establishment."

Mortified, the rope left, but spying yet another pub it decided to try again, and this time it would not be turned down. Tangling itself up and vigorously rubbing both of its ends together, several times, it marched boldly into the pub saying loudly, "A pint of your best bitter, please landlord."

"Wait a minute" the landlord said, "Aren't you a rope?"

"No," replied the rope, "I'm a frayed knot."

A man with an enormous two foot newt on his shoulder walks into a bar and says, "A pint of lager for me, and a cola for Tiny, please."

The barman gives him the drinks and takes his money, whilst all the while staring at the enormous beast. Then he says, "Why on earth do you call him 'Tiny'?"

"Because he's my newt" the man replies.

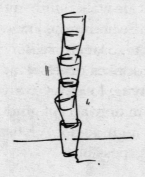

One day a man comes home from work to discover that his wife has bought him a dog. Expecting a large, lively sort of dog, he is quite happy about this until he sees that she's actually bought him a Pekinese. He takes it out for a walk anyway and bumps into a friend who is off for a drink at his local. Feeling in need of cheering up, he decides to join him. When they get to the pub, he sees a sign on the door saying, 'NO DOGS EXCEPT GUIDE DOGS'.

"Oh, bugger!" he says, looking daggers at the dog.

"Don't panic," says his friend, "We'll pretend it is a guide dog!"

"That won't work, just look at it, it's a bloody Pekinese! You don't get guide Pekinese, do you?"

"Leave this to me." said his friend, grabbing the dog's lead. He walks stiffly into the pub, up to the bar which he bumps into, slightly, and says, "Two pints of lager, please."

The landlord takes one look at the dog and says, "Sorry, mate, I can't serve you with that dog in here. We only accept guide dogs."

"But this is a guide dog," he says, trying to look as blind as possible.

"Oh, no it's not. They're all labradors or alsatians. No other dogs can learn how to do it."

"Oh my God!" shouts the friend, blindly reaching down for the dog. "What've they given me? What've they given me?"

A man walks into a bar and slaps down a pair of jump leads. The barman frowns at him and says, "Hey, don't you be trying to start anything in here."

A man walks into a bar with his pet monkey. When he gets up to the bar he sits the monkey down and asks the barman to serve his monkey a beer. The barman replies, "I am not going to serve a monkey in my bar".

After some convincing the barman agrees to give the monkey a beer. When the monkey finishes drinking the beer, he is drunk and begins to run around the bar and gets into everything that he can. Finally the monkey jumps up onto the pool table, grabs the cue ball and swallows it.

The barman, who is very upset by this time informs the customer that he will have to pay for the cue ball that his monkey has just swallowed. After some convincing, the man assures the barman that the monkey will pass the ball and he will then return it to the bar in just a few days.

As promised, a few days later the man returns with his monkey, this time on a leash, and gives the barman the cue ball back. He then asks the barman if he will once again serve his monkey a beer.

To this the barman replies, "Hell NO, the last time I did that the monkey got drunk and damn near destroyed my bar". The customer reminded the barman that the monkey is now on a leash and cannot get away from him.

After some thought the barman agrees to give the monkey a beer. The monkey sits down on the bar and begins to drink his beer. While sitting on the bar the monkey reaches over and pulls the bowl of peanuts over to him and one by one begins to eat them. Each time he picks up a peanut the monkey sticks the nut up his bottom then pulls it out and eats it. He does this several times before the barman asks, "What the hell is your monkey doing, why does he stick the peanuts up his ass before he eats them?" The man replies, "After that cue ball incident he likes to size up his meals before he eats them."

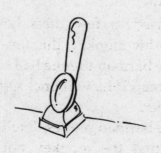

A bacon sandwich walks into a pub. He's feeling tired and run-down, and has had a dreadful day at work.

He goes up to the bar and says, "Can I have a pint of bitter, please?"

To which the barman replies, "Sorry, we don't serve food."

HEALTH WARNINGS

The doctor was trying very hard to persuade Josh to give up drinking. "Have you ever noticed a cactus plant?" he asked the heavy boozer. "If you pour water round its roots it thrives, turns greener and grows bigger. If, however, you pour alcohol on it, what happens? It shrivels, turns brown, and dies. Doesn't this teach you anything, Josh?"

"Yes, Doctor," said Josh, "it teaches me that if I want a large cactus growing in my stomach, I should drink plenty of water!"

Suggestions for when they put health warnings on alcohol...

WARNING: Consumption of alcohol is a major factor in dancing like an idiot.

WARNING: Consumption of alcohol may lead you to believe that ex-lovers are really dying for you to telephone them at four in the morning.

WARNING: Consumption of alcohol may cause you to tell the same boring story over and over again until your friends want to smash your head in.

WARNING: Consumption of alcohol may cause you to thay shings like thish.

WARNING: Consumption of alcohol may cause you to tell your boss what you really think about him while photocopying your backside at the office Christmas party.

WARNING: Consumption of alcohol may leave you wondering what on earth happened to your knickers anyway.

WARNING: Consumption of alcohol is the leading cause of inexplicable rug burn on the forehead.

WARNING: Consumption of alcohol may create the illusion that you are tougher, more handsome, and smarter than some really, really huge biker bloke named 'Big Al'.

DIAGNOSTIC TESTS...

SYMPTOM: Drinking fails to give taste and satisfaction, beer is unusually pale and clear.
FAULT: Glass empty.
ACTION: Find someone who will buy you another beer.

SYMPTOM: Drinking fails to give taste and satisfaction, and the front of your shirt is wet.
FAULT: Mouth not open when drinking or glass applied to wrong part of face.
ACTION: Buy another beer and practise in front of mirror. Drink as many as needed to perfect drinking technique.

SYMPTOM: Feet warm and wet.
FAULT: Improper bladder control.
ACTION: Go stand next to nearest dog. After a while complain to the owner about its lack of house training and demand a beer as compensation.

SYMPTOM: Floor blurred.

FAULT: You are looking through bottom of empty glass.

ACTION: Find someone who will buy you another beer.

SYMPTOM: Floor swaying.

FAULT: Excessive air turbulence, perhaps due to air-hockey game in progress.

ACTION: Insert broom handle down back of jacket.

SYMPTOM: Floor moving.

FAULT: You are being carried out.

ACTION: Find out if you are being taken to another pub. If not, complain loudly that you are being kidnapped.

SYMPTOM: Opposite wall covered with ceiling tiles and fluorescent light strip across it.

FAULT: You have fallen over backward.
ACTION: If your glass is full and no one is standing on your drinking arm, stay put. If not, get someone to help you get up; latch self to bar.

SYMPTOM: Everything has gone dim, mouth full of cigarette butts.
FAULT: You have fallen forward.
ACTION: See above.

SYMPTOM: Everything has gone dark.
FAULT: The pub is closing.
ACTION: Panic.

SYMPTOM: You awake to find your bed hard, cold and wet. You cannot see anything in your bedroom.
FAULT: You have spent the night in the gutter.
ACTION: Check your watch to see if the pubs are open yet. If not, treat yourself to a lie in.

GREAT

DRINKING

QUOTES

Catherine Zandonella
"Time is never wasted when you're wasted all the time."

Ambrose Bierce
Abstainer: a weak person who yields to the temptation of denying himself a pleasure.

W.C. Fields
"I never drink anything stronger than gin before breakfast".

"A woman drove me to drink and I didn't even have the decency to thank her."

"What contemptible scoundrel has stolen the cork to my lunch? "

"Beauty lies in the hands of the beerholder.

"Reality is an illusion that occurs due to the lack of alcohol."

Lady Astor to Winston Churchill:
"Sir, if you were my husband, I would poison your drink."
Winston Churchill to Lady Astor:
"Madam, if you were my wife, I would drink it."

Henny Youngman
"When I read about the evils of drinking, I gave up reading."

"Life is a waste of time, time is a waste of life, so get wasted all of the time and have the time of your life."

Tom Waits
"I'd rather have a bottle in front of me, than a frontal lobotomy."

"24 hours in a day, 24 beers in a case. Coincidence?"

Oscar Wilde

"Work is the curse of the drinking classes."

Dorothy Parker

"One more drink and I'd be under the host."

Humphrey Bogart

"The problem with the world is that everyone is a few drinks behind."

"Draft beer, not people!"

David Moulton

"Why is American beer served cold? So you can tell it from urine."

THE COMPUTER FREAK'S GUIDE TO BEERS...

DOS Beer: Requires you to use your own can opener, and requires you to read the directions carefully before opening the can. Originally only came in an 8-oz. can, but now comes in a 16-oz. can. However, the can is divided into 8 compartments of 2 oz. each, which have to be accessed separately. Soon to be discontinued, although a lot of people are going to keep drinking it after it's no longer available.

MAC Beer: At first, came only a 16-oz. can, but now comes in a 32-oz. can. Considered by many to be a "light" beer. All the cans look identical. When you take one from the fridge, it opens itself. The ingredients list is not on the can. If you call to ask about the ingredients, you are told that "you don't need to know." A notice on the side reminds you to drag your empties to the wastebasket. Anyone drinking it regularly will insist it is THE best beer. Even if they have never tried any other beer.

Windows 3.1 Beer: The world's most popular. Comes in a 16-oz. can that looks a lot like Mac Beer's. Requires that you already own a DOS Beer. Claims that it allows you to drink several DOS Beers simultaneously, but in reality you can only drink a few of them, very slowly, especially slowly if you are drinking the Windows Beer at the same time. Sometimes, for apparently no reason, a can of Windows Beer will explode when you open it.

OS/2 Beer: Comes in a 32-oz can. This does allow you to drink several DOS Beers simultaneously. Allows you to drink Windows 3.1 Beer simultaneously too, but somewhat slower. Advertises that its cans won't explode when you open them, even if you shake them up. You never really see anyone drinking OS/2 Beer, but the manufacturer (International Beer Manufacturing) claims that 9 million six-packs have been sold.

Windows 95 Beer: The can looks a lot like Mac Beer's can, but tastes more like Windows 3.1 Beer. It comes in 32-oz. cans, but when you look inside, the cans only have 16 oz. of beer in them. Most people will probably keep drinking Windows 3.1 Beer until their friends try Windows 95 Beer and say they like it. The ingredients list, when you look at the small print, has some of the same ingredients that come in DOS beer, even though the manufacturer claims that this is an entirely new brew.

Windows NT Beer: Comes in 32-oz. cans, but you can only buy it by the lorry load. This causes most people to have to go out and buy bigger refrigerators. The can looks just like Windows 3.1 Beer's, but the company promises to change the can to look just like Windows 95 Beer's. Touted as an "industrial strength" beer, and suggested only for use in bars.

Unix Beer: Comes in several different brands, in cans ranging from 8 oz. to 64 oz. Drinkers of Unix Beer display fierce brand loyalty, even though they claim that all the different brands taste almost identical. Sometimes the pop-tops break off when you try to open them, so you have to have your own can opener around for those occasions. In that case you either need a complete set of instructions, or a friend who has been drinking Unix Beer for several years.

Amiga Beer: The company has gone out of business, but their recipe has been picked up by some weird German company, so now this beer will be an import. This beer never really sold very well because the original manufacturer didn't understand marketing. Like Unix Beer, Amiga Beer fans are an extremely loyal and loud group. It originally came in a 16-oz. can, but now comes in 32-oz. cans too. When this can was originally introduced, it appeared flashy and colourful, but the design hasn't changed much over the years, so it appears dated now. Critics of this beer claim that it is only meant for watching TV anyway.

VMS Beer: Requires minimal user interaction, except for popping the top and sipping. However cans have been known on occasion to explode, or contain extremely un-beer-like contents.

Best drunk in high pressure development environments. When you call the manufacturer for the list of ingredients, you're told that is proprietary and you are referred to an unknown listing in manuals published by the MOD.

Rumours are that this was once listed in the GP's' Desk Reference as a tranquillizer, but no one can claim to have actually seen it.